I0058139

Awaken the Power Within

–

Leadership and Mindset Transformation

Written by Paolo Ben Salmi

Awaken the Power Within - Leadership and Mindset Transformation

Written by Paolo Ben Salmi

Adventurous
PUBLISHING

Published by Adventurous Publishing House

Interior and cover design by Lashai Ben Salmi

Paperback ISBN: 978-1-915862-78-5

Hardback ISBN: 978-1-915862-79-2

Written by Paolo Ben Salmi

Dedication

This book is dedicated to every young leader in *Africa, Middle East, Asia* and beyond who dares to dream big, to rise above challenges, and to lead with integrity and purpose. *May you embrace your power, transform your communities, and build legacies that inspire generations.*

Acknowledgements

I am so deeply grateful to my family, friends, mentors, and all those who have walked this leadership journey with me… offering wisdom, encouragement, and guidance. Special thanks to the inspiring work of Dr. Myles Munroe, whose kingdom principles continue to illuminate the path for leaders worldwide. To *you*, the reader of this book, thank you for trusting me as your companion on this transformational journey. ***Together***, we are shaping ***a brighter future***.

Table of Contents

Introduction

Welcome to *Awaken the Power Within - Leadership and Mindset Transformation*. This book isn't just about becoming better. It's about becoming *who you were created to be*. In a world full of noise, comparison, and surface-level success, I invite you to dig deeper… to discover the Kingdom principles, mindset tools, and leadership truths that awaken your true potential.

From a young age, I chose the road less traveled… guided by faith, family, and a mission bigger than myself. With influences like my mum (Sabrina), siblings (Lasha, Tray-Sean, Yasmine and Amire), Dr. Myles Munroe, mentors, Tony Evens, Dr Wayne Dyer, Regan Hillyer, David Pappoe Jr, NJ Ayuk, Clarence Seedorf, Asha Lalai, Mahamoud (Abdou) Abderamane, John Haman, Alan Shelton and a firm foundation in character and purpose, I have come to learn that real power doesn't come from titles, money, or fame. It comes from within. It's the courage to lead when no one's watching. The clarity to think beyond limits. The consistency to live for impact, not applause.

This book offers more than inspiration… It offers a blueprint. Across 20 chapters, you'll uncover practical steps, real-life stories, mindset shifts, and legacy-building habits that will help you:

- Lead with confidence, whether you're 10-years-old or 110-years-old

- Master your mindset and eliminate limiting beliefs

- Live out your faith through purpose-filled action

- Develop unshakable character in a shaky world

- Build something that outlives you

Each chapter is built on timeless truths, many rooted in the Kingdom principles taught by Dr. Myles Munroe... combined with modern insights and actionable tools. You'll find reflection points, powerful questions, and step-by-step frameworks that make leadership and mindset mastery not only possible, but ***personal***.

This is your call to rise, not someday, but today, right here and right ***now***.
Because ***you are*** the message.
You are the legacy in motion.
And the power to change your world is already within ***you***.

Let's unlock it... ***together***.

Written by Paolo Ben Salmi

CHAPTER 1

Awakening the Power Within

In a world full of distraction, confusion, and competing voices, *awakening your inner power begins with clarity of mind and purpose*. You were created with Kingdom identity, not by titles or positions, but by divine design. Before you can lead others, you must first lead *yourself*, your thoughts, emotions, and actions.

My journey began as a young dreamer with a restless spirit and a hunger to make a difference. I discovered that leadership isn't given... it's discovered. Through mentorship, prayer, reflection, solitude and Kingdom principles, I learned that true empowerment begins with knowing *who* you are in Christ and *why* you exist.

Dr. Myles Munroe taught us: *"Purpose is the reason for your existence, vision is the picture of your future, and value is the quality of your contribution."* These three truths shifted the way I saw success, not as wealth or recognition, but as *Kingdom impact*. Your value isn't what you do, it's found in who *you are becoming*.

But knowing your identity isn't enough. You also need a battle-tested mindset: one that rejects fear, embraces courage, and moves forward even when circumstances oppose you. With every setback, you are being prepared for a greater assignment. Setback is a setup for a comeback, but only if your mind is aligned to belief, not emotion.

This chapter isn't just theory, it's a practical introduction to life transformation. You'll learn simple yet profound tools to capture your thoughts, direct your emotions, and anchor your focus on purpose. With consistent daily choices, you'll begin to see a shift... from reactive living to **Kingdom intentionality**.

Remember, awakening your power isn't a one-time event... **it's a lifelong journey of renewing your mind and stewarding your gifts**. Are you ready to shift from potential to purpose? If so, then simply continue to read...

Let's begin.

Tips

- Start each morning with a 2-minute declaration of your identity for example "I am more than a conqueror", "I can do all things through Christ who strengthens me", "I am the head, not the tail", "Better days are ahead of me" and "I can be, do and have all things when I first seek the Kingdom of God" etc..
- Limit negative or toxic input such as social media, news, keep conversations to under 30 minutes daily.
- Read or listen to Kingdom-centered (or within your faith/belief system) content for at least five minutes each morning.

Techniques

1. Purchase a notepad and call it what I like to term as a "Thought Capture Journal" so you can take note of your internal dialogues: "I can't…" vs. "I can…" etc.
2. Refocus Process - Use a 5-second reset (breathe, name your purpose, continue).
3. Visualise - Write down one dream each morning; by evening, name just one small progress step that you have taken towards your dream during the day.

Action Steps

- Write a 2–sentence mission statement aligned to ***Kingdom impact***.
- Identify one negative thought you'll replace today with a positive counteractive statement that is pure truth.
- Speak out aloud to yourself at least òne positive affirmation in the mirror.

Exercises & Daily Tasks

- Evening Reflection: Identify a moment you mastered your thoughts and how did you feel?
- Accountability Partner: Share your mission statement with a member of your family, or a friend and check in with them weekly to keep you on track.
- Record a Dream Video: Describe your dream and why it matters… review it monthly.

The question is… in life are you watching the movie, are you in the movie, are you directing the movie or are you producing the movie?

The Importance of Hiring a Mentor

A mentor accelerates your journey from intention to impact. They've walked the path before, navigated obstacles, and seen pitfalls. Hiring a mentor is an investment in your Kingdom calling… someone who can speak truth, offer course corrections, and propel you forward with accountability and prayerful insight.

Quote from Paolo Ben Salmi

"Your purpose is not found in the noise… it's uncovered when you stop the noise and listen to your heart's assignment. Stop following a compass your entire life, the real compass is inside of you and it is your heart." Paolo Ben Salmi

Key Takeaways

- Identity precedes impact… you lead most powerfully when you know *who you are in the Kingdom*.
- Mindset determines direction… capture thoughts and refocus daily toward purpose.
- Consistency wins… tiny daily disciplines create monumental life shifts.
- Mentorship matters… seek guidance from someone who's further along on the journey.

CHAPTER 2

The Kingdom Mindset

Leadership isn't just about position, it's about perception. The greatest leaders don't lead because they were told to; they lead because they see the world differently. Their vision is rooted in **Kingdom principles**... It is what I like to call the **Kingdom Mindset**. It's not defined by trends or titles, but by an unshakable foundation of values, truth, and vision.

Dr. Myles Munroe said, *"You were born to lead, but to lead you must think differently."* The **Kingdom Mindset** teaches you that no matter where you're starting from, **you are royalty... meant to reign,** not simply survive. This kind of thinking shifts you from a poverty mentality to a purpose mentality. It trains you to look at problems and see potential.

Too many young people today are walking around with a survival mindset, conditioned by systems of lack, fear, guilt, shame, scarcity, loneliness, abandonment or rejection etc. But, God didn't create you to shrink back. He created you to **expand**, multiply, and steward. The **Kingdom Mindse**t is a daily decision to reject lies and **anchor your thinking to your divine assignment**.

Leadership starts in the mind. *How you think shapes how you act, and how you act shapes what you become*. When you train your brain to align with Kingdom truth, you begin to operate not from fear or pressure, but *from purpose*. Leadership without the *Kingdom mindset* will always lead to burnout. But *when your mind is renewed, your energy is restored*.

As I grew into leadership, I discovered that I had to rewire my own thoughts. Instead of saying *"I'm too young,"* I began to say *"I am uniquely positioned."* Instead of thinking *"I don't have enough,"* I reminded myself that *vision attracts provision.* Your mind is your most powerful battlefield… *win there, and you win everywhere*.

What would happen if you truly believed you were born for greatness?

What if you trained your mind to see opportunities where others see limits?

The *Kingdom Mindset* isn't just *inspiration…*

It's a discipline. Let's build it, one thought at a time.

Tips

- Start each day with a *truth statement* for example "I have the mind of a leader."
- Eliminate language of limitation for example "I can't," "I'm just…".
- Visualise yourself as a leader… how does it look, feel, and sound?

Techniques

1. **Scripture Anchoring:** Write down one Bible (or from what aligns with your own faith background) verse that aligns with Kingdom leadership and repeat it daily.
2. **Belief Board:** Create a vision board of who you are becoming as a leader.
3. **Language Shift Practice:** Write down one limiting belief per day and reframe it with a powerful counter belief.

Action Steps

- Identify three limiting beliefs and rewrite them into power statements.
- Write your ***Kingdom Mindset Manifesto,*** which is a short list of what you believe, why you believe it, and how you will live it.
- Share your manifesto with one of your peers or a mentor and ask for feedback.

Exercises & Daily Tasks

- **Journal Prompt:** Ask yourself "What belief has been holding me back and what Kingdom truth can replace it?"
- **Reflection Time:** Sit in 10 minutes of silence to ask yourself: *"What am I believing today about myself?"*
- **Mirror Exercise:** Stand in front of a mirror and say out aloud your new belief statements to yourself each morning and evening.

The Importance of Hiring a Mentor

When it comes to renewing your mindset, a mentor helps expose your blind spots. They can see where you're thinking small and where you're feeling stuck. A **Kingdom mentor** not only believes in you, but helps you *believe in yourself*. Their perspective stretches your own and that's where transformation begins.

Quote from Paolo Ben Salmi

"The most powerful kingdom you will ever lead is the one between your ears. Rule it with truth."
Paolo Ben Salmi

Key Takeaways

- Your thoughts shape your leadership capacity.
- The ***Kingdom Mindset*** is about aligning your thoughts with ***truth, purpose, and impact***.
- Small daily belief shifts create long-term leadership growth.
- A mentor can help expand your mental territory and guide you into your true calling.

CHAPTER 3

Leadership Begins With Character

When we think of leadership, we often imagine charisma, influence, and/or status. But real leadership is not about what's seen, it's about what's *built within*. And what is built first is character. Dr. Myles Munroe said, *"The foundation of leadership is character, not charisma."* Without strong character, leadership will collapse under pressure.

I learned early in life that how you treat people when no one is watching is more important than how you act on a stage. Leadership begins not with *authority*, but with **authenticity**. If you want to make an impact, start by asking: ***Am I trustworthy? Am I consistent? Do I live what I say?***

In today's world, many young people are pressured to perform before they're prepared in their character. But when you chase influence without character, you set yourself up to fail and then fall. ***Character is the root; success is the fruit. If the root is weak, no matter how high you climb, everything becomes unstable.***

So what is character, really? Character is the moral structure that holds up your life. It's integrity, honesty, humility, and accountability. It's the ability to choose what is right, even when no one else can see you and when it's uncomfortable or unpopular.

And it's a decision you make every single day, not just once.

I've faced many moments where shortcuts looked tempting, where telling the truth was harder than staying silent, or where doing the right thing cost me an opportunity. But I chose character, and in the end, I gained peace, confidence, and trust. You can't fake character… it always shows.

If you want to lead with power, start by leading with purity. Build a reputation not for being perfect, but for being *real*. The world needs young leaders whose integrity can withstand the test of time. That's how Kingdom leaders are made.

Tips

- Keep your promises, even the small ones.
- Say "I don't know" or "I was wrong" when necessary, it builds credibility.
- Guard your private life. Who you are when no one's watching matters most.

Techniques

1. **Integrity Check** – Each night, journal one moment where you upheld or compromised your values.
2. **The Mirror Test** – Can you look yourself in the eye and be proud of how you handled the day?
3. **Non-Negotiables List** – Write out 5 values that are *non-negotiable* in your life and leadership.

Action Steps

- Create a personal "code of honor" with 3–5 rules you live by.
- Practice one random act of honesty and kindness for example, return something you didn't pay for, admit a mistake. Say or do something kind for a total stranger/member of your family/friend.
- Find a mentor, member of your family or peer who can hold you accountable to your code.

Exercises & Daily Tasks

- **Morning Reflection**: Choose one character trait for example patience, discipline to practice intentionally throughout your day.
- **Evening Audit**: Did you act in alignment with your values today? If not, what will you change tomorrow?
- **Weekly Challenge**: Choose a temptation to resist this week, no matter who's watching.

The Importance of Hiring a Mentor

A mentor with integrity will sharpen your character like iron sharpens iron. They won't just tell you what you want to hear.., they'll tell you what you *need* to hear. Mentors help you identify blind spots and reinforce your values. When your character is tested, their wisdom becomes your shield.

Quote from Paolo Ben Salmi

"Character is the passport to every room your talent can't open and the anchor when storms try to drag you under." Paolo Ben Salmi

Key Takeaways

- Charisma can attract attention, but character earns trust.
- Leadership without character is dangerous.
- Building integrity takes time, but it pays lifelong dividends.
- Daily choices form your leadership legacy… start today.

CHAPTER 4

Leading Yourself First

Leadership isn't about titles or having followers. At its core, leadership is about *influence*, and the first person you must *influence* is *yourself*. Before you can lead a team, an organisation, or a movement... you must first be able to direct your thoughts, habits, emotions, and decisions.

Dr. Myles Munroe once said, *"You must be a leader of yourself before you can lead others."* That means taking ownership of your life, your mindset, your time, and your responsibilities. Too many young people want the crown but don't want the cross that comes with *discipline*.

Self-leadership requires brutal honesty. It means asking yourself hard questions:

- *Am I reliable?*
- *Am I consistent?*
- *Do I follow through on my commitments?*

Your ability to lead others is directly tied to your ability to *follow your own principles*. If you can't *lead yourself out of procrastination, distraction, or fear,* you're not ready to lead others.

This chapter is about getting real. It's about building internal discipline, emotional intelligence, and personal alignment. The battlefield isn't out there, it's in your mind. Your thoughts drive your actions, and your actions build your future. Lead your mind, or it will lead you somewhere you don't want to go.

Leading yourself also means knowing your strengths and weaknesses. You don't need to be perfect, but you do need to be intentional. Take ownership of your daily habits, your learning, your wellness, and your relationships. ***You are the CEO of your life. The results are your responsibility.***

When I started holding myself to higher standards, I noticed everything around me changed. ***I stopped blaming and started building.*** That's when leadership became real to me, not because someone called me a leader, but because I could feel the difference in how I moved, chose, and lived. ***You can feel it too.***

Tips

- Start your day with intention, not reaction.
- Write your goals down and review them daily.
- Eliminate distractions, especially those that don't serve your growth.

Techniques

1. **The 15-Minute Rule** – Commit to 15 minutes of discipline… 15 minutes of exercise, 15 minutes of journaling, 15 minutes of reading even when you feel unmotivated. Often, getting started is the hardest part.
2. **Mindset Mastery** – Begin each day with an empowering affirmation that reflects who you are becoming.
3. **Accountability Partner** – Share your weekly goals with someone who will check in with you regularly.

Action Steps

- Make a personal growth plan. Choose one skill or habit to master in the next 30 days.
- Track your daily habits. Use a calendar or habit tracker app to stay consistent.
- Identify one area where you lack self-leadership for example time management, health, focus and create a 7-day challenge to improve it.

Exercises & Daily Tasks

- **Morning Focus:** Write 3 intentions for the day that align with your bigger vision.
- **Evening Audit:** Reflect on how you led yourself today. What did you do well? What needs improving?
- **Weekly Discipline Challenge:** Choose one habit to *commit to daily* this week… *NO EXCUSES!*...

The Importance of Hiring a Mentor

Mentors help you sharpen your focus, remove excuses, and challenge your self-imposed limits. A great mentor won't just cheer you on, they'll hold up a mirror so you can lead yourself more effectively. They help turn potential into purpose.

Quote from Paolo Ben Salmi

"Before I ever stood in front of a crowd, I had to learn to stand up to my own excuses.
Self-leadership is the first victory." Paolo Ben Salmi

Key Takeaways

- You are your first follower, so *lead yourself with purpose.*
- Small habits shape big destinies.
- Self-leadership is about discipline, mindset, and ownership.
- Consistency beats motivation. *Be consistent even when you're not inspired.*

CHAPTER 5

The Power of Vision

Every great leader in history had one thing in common: vision. *Not just sight, but insight.* Dr. Myles Munroe once said, *"Sight is a function of the eyes, but vision is a function of the heart."* A true leader doesn't just see what *is*, they see what *could be*. Vision gives direction to your potential and meaning to your movement.

As a young person growing up in a fast-moving, often confusing world, you might feel like the future is foggy. But inside you lies a divine blueprint… *a dream, an idea, a fire that won't go away.* That's **your vision speaking.** *Your job is to listen, nurture it, and start walking toward it one step at a time.*

When I began visualising my future, everything changed. *I stopped reacting to life and started designing it. I stopped asking "what now?" and started asking "what next?".* A powerful vision doesn't just guide your actions, it **attracts the right people, resources, and opportunities to support you.**

Vision protects you from distraction. Without it, anything looks like the way, which can lead you down the wrong path. But with it, you can say no to what doesn't align and yes to what does. That's leadership: choosing not what's easy, but *what is aligned*. Vision gives you the courage to move even when others don't see what you see.

Whether your vision is to lead in the energy sector, technology, health, education or social impact, the first step is to write it down. Don't worry about how it will happen. Clarity creates confidence. *The 'how' shows up when the 'why' is strong enough.* Vision is your compass in uncertain times. *Why follow an external compass your entire life, when the real compass is inside of you and it is your heart... let it guide you because it already knows the way.*

Every person is born with a vision for something greater. *It's your responsibility to uncover it, protect it, and act on it.* The world is waiting for what only *you* can see. *And when you walk in vision, you don't just create change... you become it.*

Tips

Write your vision in the present tense, as if it's already real.

Read it aloud daily to program your mind with clarity.

Break your big vision into smaller goals you can work toward now.

Techniques

1. **Vision Board** – Cut out images, quotes, and goals that align with your dream life. Place it where you can see it every day.
2. **Future Letter** – Write a letter from your future self (5 years ahead), describing the life you're living and the challenges you overcame.
3. **Clarity Walks** – Take 15 minutes alone each week to walk, pray, or reflect on your vision without distractions.

Action Steps

- Write a one-sentence vision statement that starts with: "I am the kind of person who..."
- Choose three short-term goals that align with your long-term vision.
- Share your vision with someone who will support and challenge you to stay focused.

Exercises & Daily Tasks

- **Morning Affirmation:** "I am moving toward my vision daily, with purpose and faith."
- **Evening Reflection:** "What did I do today that moved me closer to my vision?"
- **Weekly Focus Challenge:** Pick one distraction to remove this week and one action that moves your vision forward.

The Importance of Hiring a Mentor

A mentor sees what you might not see yet and they remind you when you forget. They've walked the road before and help you avoid potholes along the way. A good mentor not only guides your vision but helps you *guard* it from fear, doubt, and distraction.

Quote from Paolo Ben Salmi

"Vision is your internal GPS. You may not know every turn, but if you stay connected, you'll never get lost." Paolo Ben Salmi

Key Takeaways

- Vision is the seed of leadership. Without it, you're just wandering.
- Don't wait for clarity… write, speak, and walk your vision daily.
- Vision protects you from distraction and pulls you through difficulty.
- The clearer your vision, the greater your power.

CHAPTER 6

The Silent Power of Discipline

Discipline isn't flashy, it rarely gets applause. But behind every powerful leader, every great achievement, and every lasting legacy is this silent force. *Discipline is doing what must be done, even when you don't feel like it.* It's waking up early, staying consistent, and keeping promises to yourself when no one is watching.

As a young leader, your dreams will test you. It's not your motivation but your discipline that will carry you through dark days, distractions, and doubts. The most successful people aren't the smartest, they're the ones who refused to quit. **Discipline bridges the gap between where you are and where you want to be.**

Dr. Myles Munroe taught that *true leadership is about self-discipline before it's about influence.* If you can't lead yourself, you can't lead others. This is where greatness begins, not in public, but in private. Discipline in your thoughts, your words, and your actions forms the foundation for sustainable success.

Without discipline, vision remains a dream. With it, vision becomes reality. Every habit you build is a **step toward your purpose.** The little things like reading one page a day, waking up early, limiting screen time compound into massive impact over time. Success is built in silence and revealed in results.

Discipline also protects your energy. *It tells you what to say yes to and what to walk away from.* It helps you avoid quick fixes and focus on long-term value. When you practice discipline, you gain clarity. You stop wasting energy on what doesn't align with your purpose.

The question is if you were to be very honest with yourself, at this very moment what is the truth about what you currently practice? Do you practice joy? Do you practice love? Do you practice lying? Do you practice dishonesty? Do you practice discipline? Do you practice your faith? The truth is whatever you practice, you will become good at it. At the end of the day, only the truth shall set you FREE.

Don't mistake discipline for punishment. It's an act of love - for your future, your calling, and the people you're destined to impact. When you become disciplined, you become dangerously focused, grounded, and ready to handle what most people avoid. *That's the kind of leadership Africa, the Middle East, Asia and the entire world needs.*

Tips

- Set daily routines to make your success automatic.
- Reward discipline, not just results... focus on consistency.
- Remove triggers that lead to distractions or poor habits.

Techniques

1. The Rule of One – Master one discipline at a time for example reading 15 minutes daily or exercising for 15 minutes etc before adding more.
2. Temptation Elimination – Remove things from your environment that pull you away from your goals for example unnecessary apps, sugar, time-wasters etc.
3. The 5-Minute Rule – If it takes less than five minutes and aligns with your goals, do it now to build momentum.

Action Steps

- Choose one habit to start practicing daily for the next 21 days.
- Write a "Discipline Contract", a short pledge to yourself and sign it.

- Find an accountability partner to check in with weekly.

Exercises & Daily Tasks

- **Morning Routine Practice:** Wake up 30 minutes earlier and use the time for self-growth.
- **Evening Review:** What discipline did I practice well today? Where can I improve tomorrow?
- **Discipline Journal:** Track your daily progress and write what you learn through the process.

The Importance of Hiring a Mentor

A mentor keeps your discipline alive when your motivation fades. They help you measure what matters, stay consistent when it's hard, and remind you why you started. Their discipline becomes a mirror for yours, that's how legacies are built.

Quote from Paolo Ben Salmi

"Discipline isn't about control, it's about freedom.
The more you master yourself, the more life opens
up to you." Paolo Ben Salmi

Key Takeaways

- Discipline is the bridge between goals and achievement.
- Without discipline, vision fades and distractions grow.
- Build habits that serve your future and start small.
- True leadership begins with self-leadership.

CHAPTER 7

Written by Paolo Ben Salmi

Mastering Emotional Intelligence

Emotional Intelligence (EI) *is the ability to understand and manage your emotions and those of others.* ***It's a critical skill for leaders*** *because leadership isn't about authority; it's about influence. You cannot inspire or guide others if you're overwhelmed by your own feelings or misunderstand the emotions around you.*

Many young people think intelligence is only about IQ, but Dr. Myles Munroe emphasised character and emotional maturity as the pillars of true leadership. ***EI allows you to build better relationships, communicate effectively, and make wiser decisions even under pressure.*** *It's the secret sauce behind* ***resilient leadership***.

The first step in developing EI is to develop your ***self-awareness,*** knowing your emotional triggers, recognising patterns, and understanding how your moods impact your actions. When you understand yourself deeply, you stop reacting impulsively and start responding thoughtfully. This is the difference between a child and a mature leader.

Next is ***self-regulation...*** learning to manage your emotions rather than letting them control you. Anger, fear, and frustration are natural but must be channeled constructively. This doesn't mean suppressing feelings but mastering the art of emotional balance, which builds trust and respect among your peers and followers.

Empathy, another core element of **EI**, is the ability to see situations through others' eyes. It fuels compassion and strengthens connection. When you practice empathy, you're able to unify diverse teams, navigate conflicts, and create environments where everyone feels valued.

Developing emotional intelligence is a lifelong journey, but it pays dividends in leadership and life. As you grow emotionally, you become a beacon of calm, strength, and wisdom that others will naturally follow. This is the kind of leadership that can transform our entire world.

Tips

- **Practice daily emotional check-ins:** "How do I feel right now and why?"
- Pause before reacting, count to 10 or take deep breaths.
- Listen actively, focus fully on the speaker without preparing your reply.

Techniques

1. **Journaling Emotions** – Write down your feelings and the situations that triggered them.
2. **Mindfulness Meditation** – Spend 5-10 minutes daily observing your thoughts without judgment.
3. **Role Reversal** – When upset, imagine yourself in the other person's position to build empathy.

Action Steps

- Identify your three biggest emotional triggers and create strategies to manage them.
- Practice active listening in your next conversation and reflect on how it changes the interaction.
- Find one person to discuss emotional intelligence and share what you're learning.

Exercises & Daily Tasks

- **Emotion Log**: Track your emotional highs and lows throughout the day and note your responses.
- **Empathy Challenge**: Intentionally ask someone how they're feeling and listen without interrupting.
- **Self-Regulation Practice**: When upset, practice a calming technique like deep breathing or counting.

The Importance of Hiring a Mentor

A mentor who models emotional intelligence can guide you through tough emotional terrain. They provide perspective, hold you accountable for growth, and show how emotional mastery strengthens leadership. Their wisdom helps you turn emotional challenges into stepping stones.

Quote from Paolo Ben Salmi

"Emotional intelligence is the compass that guides your leadership journey… without it, you risk losing your way." Paolo Ben Salmi

Key Takeaways

- Emotional intelligence is vital for impactful leadership.
- Self-awareness and self-regulation are foundational to **EI**.
- Empathy builds connection and trust.
- **EI** is a lifelong practice that transforms relationships and leadership.

CHAPTER 8

Written by Paolo Ben Salmi

The Power of Visionary Leadership

Visionary leadership is the ability to see beyond the present and imagine a future that others may not yet understand. It's the spark that ignites progress and transformation. Dr. Myles Munroe emphasised that vision is the ability to see the invisible and make it visible. As a young leader, cultivating a clear, compelling vision will give your life and work purpose and direction.

Without vision, leadership becomes reactive and aimless. Vision empowers you to navigate challenges with confidence because you know what you're working toward. It allows you to inspire others to join your cause and to persevere when obstacles arise. Visionary leaders don't just adapt to change, they create it.

Developing visionary leadership starts with self-reflection. What are your core values? What change do you want to see in your community, industry, or continent? When your vision aligns with your purpose, your passion fuels your persistence. You become a beacon, drawing people toward a shared future.

It's important to communicate your vision clearly and consistently. Words alone won't inspire; your actions must reflect your vision daily. Dr. Munroe taught that character must support vision, without integrity and consistency, a vision loses credibility. People follow leaders they trust.

Visionary leadership also means being adaptable. The world is constantly changing, especially in Africa's, the Middle East and Asia's fast-evolving landscape. Leaders with vision are flexible enough to pivot when necessary but steadfast enough to keep their eyes on the prize. This balance of clarity and adaptability is a hallmark of great leadership.

When you lead with vision, you empower others to discover their own potential. Visionary leaders build legacies by creating more leaders, not just followers. Your vision has the power to inspire generations and drive global transformation.

Tips

- Spend time daily visualising your future success and impact.
- Write your vision statement and review it weekly.
- Share your vision with others to build momentum.

Techniques

1. **Vision Board Creation** – Use images and words to create a physical or digital board representing your goals.
2. **Future Self Meditation** – Imagine yourself 5 or 10 years ahead living your vision fully.
3. **Storytelling** – Practice telling your vision as a compelling story to inspire others.

Action Steps

- Write a clear, concise vision statement for your life or leadership role.
- Identify three ways your daily actions support your vision.
- Find a community or group that shares your vision or goals.

Exercises & Daily Tasks

- **Morning Visualization**: Spend 5 minutes envisioning your goals as if already achieved.
- **Vision Reflection Journal**: Journal about obstacles and breakthroughs related to your vision.
- **Accountability Check**: Share your vision with a mentor or peer and update them on progress monthly.

The Importance of Hiring a Mentor

Mentors help clarify your vision and hold you accountable to it. They provide wisdom to refine your direction and encouragement to stay committed when the journey gets tough. Their experience accelerates your path from vision to reality.

Quote from Paolo Ben Salmi

"A vision without action is just a dream; visionary leadership turns dreams into destiny." Paolo Ben Salmi

Key Takeaways

- Visionary leadership is essential for meaningful impact.
- A clear vision guides decision-making and inspires others.
- Character and consistency support the credibility of your vision.
- Mentorship accelerates your journey to realising your vision.

CHAPTER 9

Building Character That Leads

Character is the foundation of true leadership. Dr. Myles Munroe famously said, *"Leadership is influence, nothing more, nothing less."* But to influence others positively, your character must be trustworthy, consistent, and strong. Without character, leadership is fragile and short-lived.

Building character means committing to honesty, integrity, humility, and accountability in every area of your life. It's about doing the right thing even when no one is watching. Character is tested in moments of challenge, when you choose your values over convenience or popularity.

Youth face unique challenges that test their character daily: corruption, peer pressure, economic hardships, and social injustices. These challenges present opportunities to demonstrate resilience and ethical leadership. Choosing character empowers you to rise above circumstances and model the change that our world desperately needs.

Character shapes how you respond to failure and success alike. A leader with strong character owns mistakes, learns from them, and uses setbacks as fuel to grow. Likewise, humility in success keeps you grounded and connected to your purpose and people.

One of the keys to building character is *self-discipline...* the ability to control impulses, focus on long-term goals, and uphold your principles. Discipline is not a restriction but a pathway to freedom. It helps you avoid destructive shortcuts and maintain your integrity.

Ultimately, character attracts followers and mentors alike. People want to follow leaders they respect and trust. *Character builds a legacy that outlasts titles or positions.* As you build your character, you lay the groundwork for powerful, sustainable leadership.

Tips

- Reflect daily on your actions... did they align with your values?
- Practice honesty in small matters to strengthen integrity.
- Seek feedback from trusted peers on your character growth.

Techniques

1. **Value Clarification** – Write down your top five core values and examples of living them.
2. **Accountability Partner** – Partner with someone who will help keep you honest and disciplined.
3. **Failure Reflection** – Analyse a past mistake and write what it taught you about your character.

Action Steps

- Identify one character trait you want to develop and create a plan to practice it daily.
- Commit to one act of integrity each day, no matter how small.
- Find a role model whose character inspires you and learn from their example.

Exercises & Daily Tasks

- **Character Journal:** Record instances where you demonstrated or compromised your character.
- **Discipline Challenge:** Set a daily habit goal that requires self-control for example waking up early, avoiding distractions.

- **Reflection Time:** Spend 5 minutes nightly reviewing your actions and intentions.

The Importance of Hiring a Mentor

Mentors serve as living examples of strong character. They provide guidance on how to handle ethical dilemmas and offer honest feedback on your growth. A mentor's wisdom helps you develop character faster and avoid costly mistakes.

Quote from Paolo Ben Salmi

"Character is the silent language that speaks louder than words; it's the currency of leadership." Paolo Ben Salmi

Key Takeaways

- Character is the foundation of lasting leadership.
- Integrity, humility, and accountability build trust and influence.
- Self-discipline empowers you to uphold your values consistently.
- Mentorship accelerates character development through guidance and example.

CHAPTER 10

The Mindset Shift to Leadership

Leadership begins with mindset-the beliefs, attitudes, and perspectives that shape how you see yourself and the world around you. Without the right mindset, even the best plans and talents can fall short. Dr. Myles Munroe taught that your mindset determines your destiny; it's the lens through which you interpret challenges and opportunities.

A leadership mindset is proactive, growth-oriented, and resilient. It means embracing responsibility, seeking continuous learning, and viewing setbacks as stepping stones rather than roadblocks. The African, Middle Eastern and Asian youth face rapid change and uncertainty, making this mindset essential to navigating today's complex environment.

One key shift is from a fixed mindset, which believes abilities and intelligence are static, to a growth mindset, which sees potential for development through effort and learning. Leaders with growth mindsets empower themselves and others to push beyond limits and innovate solutions that drive transformation.

Developing a leadership mindset requires self-awareness… understanding your strengths, weaknesses, and triggers. It also involves cultivating emotional intelligence: the ability to manage your emotions and empathise with others. These qualities build trust and effective communication.

Another vital aspect is purpose-driven leadership. Knowing why you lead fuels passion and perseverance, especially when facing obstacles. Purpose anchors your vision and keeps you grounded in service to others, rather than personal gain.

Shifting your mindset to leadership is a continuous journey. It requires intentional daily practices and a supportive environment. Surround yourself with positive influences, invest in personal growth, and embrace challenges as opportunities to rise.

Tips

- Practice daily affirmations to reinforce a positive leadership mindset.
- Reflect on past failures and identify lessons learned to reframe setbacks.
- Seek feedback to grow your self-awareness and emotional intelligence.

Techniques

1. **Growth Mindset Journaling** – Write about challenges and how you can learn from them.
2. **Emotional Check-ins** – Pause several times a day to assess your emotions and reactions.
3. **Purpose Clarification** – Define your 'why' and revisit it regularly.

Action Steps

- Identify one limiting belief and replace it with an empowering one.
- Set a learning goal to acquire a new leadership skill or knowledge this month.
- Practice empathy by actively listening to someone's perspective each day.

Exercises & Daily Tasks

- **Morning Mindset Routine**: Start your day with leadership affirmations and visualisation.
- **Emotional Intelligence Practice**: Note emotional triggers and how you respond to them.
- **Purpose Reflection**: Write a short paragraph on how your leadership serves others.

The Importance of Hiring a Mentor

A mentor challenges your mindset by offering new perspectives and holding you accountable to your growth. They help you navigate blind spots and encourage resilience in moments of doubt. Their experience is a compass on your mindset shift journey.

Quote from Paolo Ben Salmi
"Leadership is born not from position, but from the mindset to serve, grow, and uplift." Paolo Ben Salmi

Key Takeaways

- Mindset shapes how you lead and respond to challenges.
- A growth and purpose-driven mindset fuels resilient leadership.
- Emotional intelligence enhances trust and communication.
- Mentors accelerate mindset shifts through guidance and accountability.

CHAPTER 11

Written by Paolo Ben Salmi

Leading with Kingdom Principles

Leadership rooted in *Kingdom principles* goes beyond personal ambition and worldly success; it is leadership grounded in eternal values that promote justice, service, and stewardship. Dr. Myles Munroe emphasised that true leadership reflects the heart of a servant, focused on building others up and advancing a greater purpose.

Kingdom leadership calls for leaders who prioritise integrity, humility, and selflessness. These qualities foster environments where people thrive, trust is cultivated, and communities flourish. We live in a world, where leadership challenges are abundant, *Kingdom principles* offer a transformative framework for impactful leadership.

Practicing *Kingdom principles* means embracing leadership as a sacred responsibility. It requires accountability not only to people but to higher standards of moral and ethical conduct. This approach restores dignity to leadership and counters corruption and selfishness that have hindered progress.

A *Kingdom leader* understands the importance of vision with purpose. Vision guided by Kingdom principles is about seeing beyond immediate gains to lasting legacy, the kind of leadership that shapes nations and inspires generations.

These principles also encourage leaders to empower others by mentoring, sharing wisdom, and creating opportunities. Kingdom leadership is inherently intergenerational and inclusive, seeking to develop potential in everyone regardless of status or background.

Ultimately, leading with Kingdom principles transforms not just organisations, but entire societies. It cultivates leaders who lead with heart, courage, and wisdom, the leaders Africa, Asia, the Middle East and our entire world so urgently needs.

Tips

- Reflect on how your leadership aligns with Kingdom values like integrity and service.
- Prioritise humility by actively listening and valuing others' contributions.
- Serve your community through acts of kindness and empowerment.

Techniques

1. **Kingdom Leadership Meditation** – Spend time daily meditating on key Kingdom values and how to embody them.

2. **Service Mapping** – Identify areas where you can serve or mentor others in your circle.
3. **Vision Alignment Exercise** – Write down your leadership vision and evaluate it against Kingdom principles.

Action Steps

- Commit to one act of servant leadership each week.
- Seek out opportunities to mentor or uplift someone younger or less experienced.
- Regularly review your leadership decisions to ensure they reflect Kingdom ethics.

Exercises & Daily Tasks

- **Daily Reflection**: Journal how you practiced humility and service today.
- **Vision Board**: Create a visual representation of your Kingdom-driven leadership goals.
- **Community Engagement**: Volunteer or participate in a local initiative weekly.

The Importance of Hiring a Mentor

A mentor who embodies Kingdom principles serves as a living example and guide. They help you navigate leadership challenges with wisdom and grace, modeling servant leadership in action. Their influence nurtures your growth into a principled, effective leader.

Quote from Paolo Ben Salmi
"Kingdom leadership is the highest calling, where influence is exercised with integrity, purpose, and love." Paolo Ben Salmi

Key Takeaways

- Kingdom principles anchor leadership in service, integrity, and vision.
- Humility and accountability are essential for transformative leadership.
- Empowerment and mentorship extend Kingdom leadership beyond self.
- Mentors guide you to embody these principles authentically and effectively.

CHAPTER 12

The Role of Character in Leadership

Character is the foundation upon which true leadership stands. It is the consistent demonstration of values, integrity, and ethical behaviour that earns trust and respect. Without strong character, leadership becomes hollow and unstable. Dr. Myles Munroe famously stated, "Leadership is not about position or title, but about character and influence."

In a world where leadership scandals often make headlines, African, Asian, Middle Eastern and our entire world youth must understand that character defines their legacy far more than achievements or accolades. A leader's actions, decisions, and how they treat others reveal their true character over time.

Developing character requires intentionality. It involves choosing honesty over convenience, humility over pride, and fairness over favouritism. Character shapes your response when no one is watching and determines how you bounce back from failures.

Leadership challenges often test character, when faced with pressure, temptation, or conflict. It is during these moments that a leader's true nature emerges. Those who cultivate strong character are better equipped to lead with consistency and earn lasting loyalty.

Character also influences culture. Leaders with integrity create environments where people feel safe, valued, and motivated to contribute their best. This ripple effect *fosters high performance* and innovation, crucial for world growth.

Ultimately, character is leadership's greatest currency. It is the invisible quality that empowers leaders to inspire, unite, and transform communities for the better.

Tips

- Commit to daily honesty and transparency in your actions.
- Practice humility by admitting mistakes and learning from them.
- Treat everyone with fairness and respect, regardless of their status.

Techniques

1. **Character Audit** – Regularly assess your actions against your core values.
2. **Accountability Partner** – Find someone to help you stay true to your commitments.
3. **Reflective Journaling** – Write about situations where your character was challenged and how you responded.

Action Steps

- Identify one area where you need to strengthen your character and create a plan for improvement.
- Seek feedback on your integrity and behaviour from trusted peers or mentors.
- Practice transparency by openly communicating intentions and decisions.

Exercises & Daily Tasks

- **Daily Integrity Check**: Reflect on choices you made and whether they aligned with your values.
- **Gratitude Practice**: Acknowledge moments where others' good character inspired you.
- **Conflict Reflection**: Analyse a recent conflict and how your character influenced the outcome.

The Importance of Hiring a Mentor

A mentor holds a mirror to your character, helping you see blind spots and providing guidance on ethical leadership. They challenge you to rise above temptations and model integrity, offering a safe space for honest reflection and growth.

Quote from Paolo Ben Salmi

"Character is the invisible currency of leadership, spend it wisely, and your legacy will be priceless."

Paolo Ben Salmi

Key Takeaways

- Character is the bedrock of credible and effective leadership.
- Integrity, humility, and fairness must be practiced consistently.
- Leadership challenges test and reveal character.
- Mentors provide accountability and guidance to nurture strong character.

CHAPTER 13

Cultivating a Kingdom Mindset for Growth

A Kingdom mindset is the perspective that prioritises eternal values over temporary gains, focusing on growth that benefits not just the individual, but communities and future generations. It is a mindset deeply rooted in purpose, faith, and stewardship… principles that Dr. Myles Munroe passionately advocated as essential for true success.

Cultivating this mindset means shifting from a scarcity mentality, where fear and competition dominate to an abundance mentality, which embraces collaboration, generosity, and long-term vision. African (Africa has the youngest population of youth under the age of 30) youth are uniquely positioned to embrace this mindset as they build the continent's future.

Growth with a Kingdom mindset is holistic. It includes personal development, spiritual maturity, relational depth, and societal impact. It is not just about career success but about becoming the best version of yourself to serve others effectively.

This mindset encourages resilience and adaptability. Challenges are seen as opportunities to learn and grow rather than obstacles to fear. It fosters a deep confidence rooted in identity and calling, not just external achievements.

Leaders with a Kingdom mindset invest in people, ideas, and innovations that uplift their communities. They understand that true legacy is built on empowering others and stewarding resources wisely.

Ultimately, cultivating a Kingdom mindset transforms how youth lead, live, and influence, equipping them to navigate complex challenges with faith, wisdom, and courage.

Tips

- Practice gratitude daily to focus on abundance rather than lack.
- Surround yourself with positive, growth-oriented people.
- Set goals that align with your purpose and values, not just material success.

Techniques

1. **Mindset Journaling** – Reflect weekly on your thoughts, beliefs, and attitudes about growth.
2. **Visualisation** – Regularly imagine the impact of your growth on yourself and your community.

3. **Affirmation Practice** – Use Kingdom-based affirmations to reinforce positive thinking.

Action Steps

- Identify limiting beliefs that hinder your growth and replace them with Kingdom truths.
- Develop a personal mission statement that reflects your Kingdom's purpose.
- Seek opportunities to mentor or be mentored to foster mutual growth.

Exercises & Daily Tasks

- **Daily Gratitude List**: Write three things you're thankful for each day.
- **Purpose Reflection**: Spend 10 minutes each morning recalling why your growth matters.
- **Growth Challenge**: Push yourself weekly to try something outside your comfort zone.

The Importance of Hiring a Mentor

Mentors provide perspective and wisdom that shape your mindset, helping you overcome self-doubt and limiting beliefs. Their experience accelerates your growth and keeps you aligned with Kingdom values during difficult seasons.

Quote from Paolo Ben Salmi
"A Kingdom mindset is the compass that guides us from mere ambition to meaningful impact."
Paolo Ben Salmi

Key Takeaways

- A Kingdom mindset prioritises purpose, abundance, and holistic growth.
- Resilience and adaptability flourish in a mindset rooted in faith and vision.
- Investing in others is central to sustainable leadership growth.
- Mentorship is vital in cultivating and sustaining a Kingdom mindset.

CHAPTER 14

The Power of Servant Leadership

Servant leadership turns the traditional leadership model upside down. Instead of seeking power and status, servant leaders focus on serving others, empowering, uplifting, and nurturing their teams and communities. Dr. Myles Munroe emphasised that true leadership is about influence, not authority, and servant leadership embodies this principle.

In Africa's, Asia's and the Middle Eastern's evolving landscape, servant leadership is crucial. Young leaders who prioritise service build trust, foster collaboration, and create environments where innovation and growth thrive. Serving others strengthens bonds and aligns leadership with a greater purpose beyond self-interest.

Servant leaders listen actively, empathise deeply, and respond with compassion. They seek to understand before seeking to be understood, creating a culture of mutual respect and inclusivity. This approach challenges ego-driven leadership styles that often lead to division and mistrust.

Embracing servant leadership means developing humility, the willingness to put others' needs before your own and to celebrate their successes genuinely. This humility breeds loyalty and inspires teams to give their best.

Servant leadership also involves sacrifice. It requires leaders to invest time, energy, and resources in the growth of others without immediate personal gain. This investment pays dividends in strong relationships and sustainable success.

Ultimately, servant leadership transforms leaders into catalysts for positive change, fostering environments where everyone can flourish and contribute meaningfully to world progress.

Tips

- Practice active listening in all your conversations.
- Prioritise the needs and growth of your team or community.
- Celebrate others' achievements and encourage collaboration.

Techniques

1. **Empathy Exercises** – Regularly put yourself in others' shoes to understand their perspectives.
2. **Gratitude Sharing** – Publicly acknowledge contributions of team members or peers.
3. **Service Projects** – Engage in community service to strengthen your servant leadership skills.

Action Steps

- Identify one person or group you can serve intentionally this week. If you are feeling ambitious you could create a weekly plan that will cover 52 weeks of servitude.
- Reflect daily on how your actions either served or self-centered your leadership.
- Create a plan to foster a culture of service within your environment.

Exercises & Daily Tasks

- **Daily Listening Challenge**: Commit to fully listening without interrupting or planning your response.
- **Acts of Kindness**: Perform one small act of service each day.
- **Reflection Journal**: Write about how serving others changed your perspective or relationships.

The Importance of Hiring a Mentor

A mentor modeling servant leadership shows by example how to lead with humility and compassion. They provide guidance on balancing authority with service and inspire you to grow beyond self-centered leadership.

Quote from Paolo Ben Salmi
"The greatest leader is first a servant, serving with humility, leading with heart." Paolo Ben Salmi

Key Takeaways

- Servant leadership focuses on empowering and uplifting others.
- Listening, empathy, and humility are core to servant leadership.
- Service requires sacrifice but yields sustainable influence and trust.
- Mentors are essential in guiding servant leaders to balance power with compassion.

CHAPTER 15

Building Resilience Through Kingdom Principles

Resilience is the ability to withstand adversity, bounce back from setbacks, and keep moving forward with determination. Dr. Myles Munroe taught that resilience is deeply connected to one's character and kingdom mindset, a faith-rooted strength that transcends circumstances.

For young leaders, especially in Africa's, the Middle East, Asia's and other parts of the world are certainly dynamic environments, resilience is not optional; it is essential. Challenges such as economic instability, social pressure, and personal trials are inevitable. Yet, by grounding ourselves in kingdom principles like purpose, integrity, and hope, we build unshakable resilience.

Resilience begins with understanding your identity and purpose. When you know who you are and why you exist, external difficulties become temporary obstacles rather than permanent roadblocks. Kingdom principles remind us that trials refine our character and prepare us for greater impact.

Practicing resilience means cultivating patience and perseverance, even when results aren't immediate. It involves trusting the process and God's timing, embracing setbacks as lessons, and refusing to give up on your vision.

Resilient leaders also lean on their community and mentors for support and encouragement. Kingdom principles emphasise unity and mutual strengthening, showing that resilience is often a collective effort.

Ultimately, building resilience through kingdom principles empowers youth to face challenges boldly, grow through hardship, and lead with unwavering faith and courage.

Tips

- Anchor yourself daily in your purpose to stay motivated during tough times.
- Practice patience by setting realistic expectations and timelines.
- Surround yourself with a supportive community and mentors.

Techniques

1. **Positive Reframing** – Challenge negative thoughts by finding lessons or opportunities in difficulties.
2. **Faith Meditation** – Spend time reflecting on kingdom promises that build hope and strength.

3. **Goal Adjustment** – Regularly reassess and adapt your goals without losing sight of your purpose.

Action Steps

- Write down your core purpose and review it each morning.
- Identify a recent challenge and list three lessons you learned from it.
- Reach out to a mentor or trusted friend when feeling overwhelmed.

Exercises & Daily Tasks

- **Daily Affirmation**: Say aloud, "I am resilient because my strength is rooted in my purpose."
- **Journaling**: Reflect on moments you overcame difficulty and what helped you persevere.
- **Support Check-In**: Schedule weekly conversations with mentors or peers for encouragement.

The Importance of Hiring a Mentor

A mentor offers perspective and encouragement that reinforce resilience. They share wisdom from their own challenges, guide you through setbacks, and remind you of kingdom truths when discouragement threatens to take hold.

Quote from Paolo Ben Salmi

"Resilience is the fruit of faith applied; it's the courage to keep walking when the path is steep and uncertain." Paolo Ben Salmi

Key Takeaways

- Resilience is a mindset built on purpose, patience, and faith.
- Challenges refine character and prepare leaders for greater impact.
- Support systems and mentors are vital for sustaining resilience.
- Kingdom principles provide the foundation for unshakable strength.

CHAPTER 16

Leading with Integrity and Character

Integrity and character form the foundation of true leadership. Dr. Myles Munroe taught that leadership is not just about position or power, but about who you are when no one is watching. The character of a leader shapes their legacy and influences the trust they build with others.

In Africa, Asia and the Middle East where young leaders face complex ethical challenges, leading with integrity becomes a revolutionary act. It means choosing honesty over convenience, accountability over shortcuts, and standing firm on your values even when pressured to compromise.

Character is developed through consistent choices, small decisions that reflect your core beliefs. It is not an overnight achievement but a lifelong commitment. When leaders embody integrity, they inspire loyalty and foster cultures of transparency and respect.

Leading with character also requires humility, the ability to admit mistakes, seek feedback, and continuously grow. This humility enhances credibility and models a learning mindset that empowers others to improve alongside you.

Ethical leadership strengthens communities and organisations. It combats corruption and builds a trustworthy reputation, which is critical for sustainable progress and meaningful impact across Africa, Asia and the Middle East.

Ultimately, leaders who prioritise integrity and character sow seeds of trust and honor that flourish far beyond their tenure, influencing generations to come.

Tips

- Always speak truthfully, even when it's difficult.
- Hold yourself accountable for your actions and decisions.
- Reflect regularly on whether your actions align with your core values.

Techniques

1. **Value Clarification** – Write down your top five core values and revisit them weekly.
2. **Integrity Check** – Before making decisions, ask yourself if you would be proud for others to know your choice.
3. **Feedback Loop** – Actively seek constructive feedback and respond with openness.

Action Steps

- Identify a situation where you compromised your integrity and write lessons learned.
- Create a personal leadership code of ethics to guide your decisions.
- Commit to transparency in your communication this week.

Exercises & Daily Tasks

- **Daily Reflection**: End each day reviewing how you upheld your values.
- **Accountability Partner**: Pair with a peer to discuss challenges to integrity.
- **Honesty Practice**: Practice delivering truthful feedback kindly and respectfully.

The Importance of Hiring a Mentor

A mentor who exemplifies integrity offers a living example of ethical leadership. They provide honest feedback, hold you accountable, and guide you through moral dilemmas with wisdom grounded in character.

Quote from Paolo Ben Salmi

"Integrity is the soul of leadership; without it, influence fades and trust crumbles." Paolo Ben Salmi

Key Takeaways

- Leadership is defined by character, not title.
- Integrity requires courage to be honest and accountable.
- Humility and openness to feedback strengthen character.
- Mentors are vital in guiding ethical leadership development.

CHAPTER 17

The Role of Vision in Leadership

Vision is the cornerstone of effective leadership. It is the ability to see beyond the present moment and imagine a future that others cannot yet perceive. Dr. Myles Munroe emphasised that vision gives purpose to leadership and ignites the passion necessary to pursue goals relentlessly.

For young African, Asian, Middle Eastern leaders, having a clear and compelling vision is essential to navigate the challenges and opportunities unique to the continent. Vision helps you stay focused amid distractions and inspires those around you to work together toward a shared goal.

A well-crafted vision aligns your actions, decisions, and resources toward a meaningful impact. It serves as a roadmap during difficult times and a motivational force that keeps you resilient when obstacles arise.

Developing vision requires intentional reflection on your passions, strengths, and the needs of your community. It's not just about personal success but about creating value that benefits others and contributes to collective progress.

Leaders with vision communicate their dreams with clarity and conviction, attracting followers who share their commitment. This creates a culture of collaboration and innovation necessary for sustainable change.

Ultimately, vision empowers leaders to transform ideas into reality, shaping the future with purpose and confidence.

Tips

- Regularly revisit and refine your vision to ensure it remains relevant and inspiring.
- Share your vision clearly with your team and stakeholders to build alignment.
- Break your vision into achievable milestones to maintain momentum.

Techniques

1. Vision Mapping – Write a detailed description of your ideal future and visualise daily.
2. SWOT Analysis – Identify Strengths, Weaknesses, Opportunities, and Threats related to your vision.
3. Vision Board Creation – Use images and words that represent your goals to keep your vision tangible.

Action Steps

- Draft a personal and/or organisational vision statement.
- Share your vision with at least three people and gather feedback.
- Set short-term goals that align directly with your vision.

Exercises & Daily Tasks

- **Morning Visualisation:** Spend five minutes imagining the successful realisation of your vision.
- **Vision Reflection Journal:** Document progress, challenges, and insights weekly.
- **Accountability Check-In:** Partner with a mentor or peer to discuss your vision progress monthly.

The Importance of Hiring a Mentor

A mentor can help refine your vision by providing perspective, challenging assumptions, and offering experience-based advice. They support you in staying focused and adapting your vision as circumstances change.

Quote from Paolo Ben Salmi

"Vision is the light that guides a leader through the storms of uncertainty." Paolo Ben Salmi

Key Takeaways

- Vision is the foundation for purposeful leadership.
- Clear communication of vision aligns and motivates teams.
- Breaking vision into milestones fosters progress.
- Mentorship enhances vision clarity and adaptability.

CHAPTER 18

The Power of Influence and Service

True leadership is measured not by authority or control but by the ability to influence others positively and serve them selflessly. Dr. Myles Munroe emphasised that leadership is about empowering others to become their best selves and fulfill their potential.

Influence is the currency of leadership. It flows from *trust, respect, and genuine care* for people's well-being. Leaders who serve their communities and teams build deep connections that inspire loyalty and collective progress.

In African, Asian, Middle Eastern contexts, where communities face diverse challenges, leaders who embrace service create meaningful impact by addressing real needs with compassion and strategic action. This servant leadership model fosters unity and resilience.

Service requires humility-a willingness to put others before yourself, listen actively, and respond thoughtfully. It transforms leadership from a position of privilege to a responsibility grounded in love and stewardship.

The power of influence combined with service drives sustainable change. Leaders who invest in uplifting others multiply their impact far beyond what individual efforts can achieve.

Ultimately, leadership through influence and service creates legacies of transformation, empowering generations to thrive and contribute to Africa's, Asia's and the Middle Eastern's flourishing future.

Tips

- Practice active listening to understand the needs of those you serve.
- Lead by example, demonstrating integrity and compassion.
- Prioritise the growth and development of your team members.

Techniques

1. **Empathy Mapping** – Identify the feelings, thoughts, and needs of those you lead.
2. **Servant Leadership Reflection** – Journal about ways you have served others and areas to improve.
3. **Influence Assessment** – Seek feedback on how your actions affect others' motivation and trust.

Action Steps

- Volunteer for a community project or cause you care about.
- Mentor someone and focus on their growth and success.
- Practice daily acts of kindness and service within your network.

Exercises & Daily Tasks

- **Gratitude Practice**: Acknowledge and thank someone you serve every day.
- **Active Listening Drill**: In conversations, focus fully on understanding before responding.
- **Service Goal**: Set a weekly goal for a service-oriented action, big or small.

The Importance of Hiring a Mentor

A mentor models how to lead with influence and serve effectively. They teach the balance of humility and strength and help you cultivate genuine relationships based on trust and respect.

Quote from Paolo Ben Salmi
"Leadership rooted in service transforms influence into lasting impact." Paolo Ben Salmi

Key Takeaways

- Leadership thrives on influence built through trust and service.
- Serving others requires humility and active listening.
- Influence combined with service multiplies leadership impact.
- Mentors demonstrate servant leadership and nurture your growth.

CHAPTER 19

Written by Paolo Ben Salmi

Building a Legacy through Leadership and Character

Legacy is the lasting impact a leader leaves behind, a footprint that influences generations beyond their lifetime. True legacy is built not on wealth or titles, but on character and the quality of leadership exhibited throughout one's life. Dr. Myles Munroe taught that leadership without character is a dangerous combination; character forms the foundation upon which meaningful legacies are built.

In Africa, Asia and the Middle East, where communities are shaped by shared values and heritage, leaders who uphold integrity, honesty, and responsibility inspire trust and admiration. Character defines how a leader makes decisions, treats others, and overcomes challenges, and this shapes how their legacy will be remembered.

Building a legacy requires consistent commitment to ethical leadership, making choices that serve the greater good even when it's difficult. This commitment fosters respect and builds credibility, allowing leaders to influence positive change far beyond their immediate environment.

Written by Paolo Ben Salmi

Character-driven leadership empowers others to adopt these values, creating a ripple effect that strengthens communities and institutions. Legacy is not just about what you achieve but about who you are and how you uplift others.

Leaders who intentionally cultivate character alongside skills and vision set the stage for sustainable impact. Their legacy becomes a beacon for future leaders to emulate and surpass.

Ultimately, building a legacy is about stewardship, responsibly managing your influence, resources, and relationships to leave a better world for those who follow.

Tips

- Reflect regularly on your values and how they align with your leadership style.
- Practice integrity in small daily decisions to build trust.
- Be accountable and transparent with your team and community.

Techniques

1. **Character Audit** – Assess your strengths and weaknesses in key character traits like honesty, patience, and humility.
2. **Legacy Visioning** – Write about the kind of legacy you want to leave and steps to get there.
3. **Accountability Partner** – Work with someone who can challenge and support your character development.

Action Steps

- Identify role models who exemplify strong character and study their leadership.
- Make a list of core values to guide your decisions and actions.
- Practice ethical decision-making in challenging situations.

Exercises & Daily Tasks

- **Daily Reflection**: Journal about moments where your character was tested and how you responded.
- **Gratitude and Apology**: Acknowledge where you've fallen short and commit to improvement.

- **Character Challenge**: Set a weekly goal to demonstrate a specific trait intentionally.

The Importance of Hiring a Mentor

A mentor with strong character models ethical leadership in action. They provide guidance on navigating moral dilemmas and reinforce the importance of values in building lasting influence.

Quote from Paolo Ben Salmi

"Legacy is the echo of your character in the hearts
of those you lead." Paolo Ben Salmi

Key Takeaways

- Legacy is built on consistent character and ethical leadership.
- Integrity and accountability foster trust and respect.
- Character-driven leaders inspire future generations.
- Mentorship supports character growth and ethical decision-making.

CHAPTER 20

The Final Message - Embracing Your Power as a Leader

As we conclude this journey together, it's vital to remember that the power of leadership lies within you. You are not defined by your circumstances, but by your choices and your willingness to rise above challenges. Dr. Myles Munroe's kingdom principles remind us that leadership is a responsibility bestowed upon those who are prepared to serve with integrity and vision.

Embracing your power means acknowledging both your strengths and weaknesses, and committing daily to growth in character, mindset, and skills. It requires courage to face fears, humility to accept guidance, and resilience to persist through setbacks.

The African continent stands at the crossroads of immense opportunity, and the youth hold the keys to its transformation. By stepping into your leadership power, you become a catalyst for change, lifting communities, inspiring others, and building a legacy of hope and progress.

True leadership is not about titles or recognition; it's about influence and service that create sustainable impact. As you lead with purpose and conviction, you contribute to a greater narrative, one that shapes the future of Africa, the Middle East. Asia and beyond.

Remember, leadership is a lifelong journey. Each day presents new chances to learn, mentor, innovate, and inspire. Embrace this journey with an open heart and a clear vision, knowing that your contribution matters deeply.

Your power as a leader is the gift you offer to the world. Own it, nurture it, and let it shine boldly, because when you lead from a place of authenticity and love, you become unstoppable.

Tips

- Embrace continuous learning and self-improvement.
- Cultivate resilience to navigate challenges.
- Lead with authenticity and compassion.

Techniques

1. **Daily Affirmations** – Reinforce your leadership identity with empowering statements.
2. **Vision Board** – Create a visual representation of your leadership goals and legacy.
3. **Mindfulness Practice** – Develop awareness to stay grounded in purpose during stress.

Action Steps

- Identify one leadership habit to develop over the next 30 days.
- Seek out opportunities to mentor or support emerging leaders.
- Reflect weekly on progress and areas for growth.

Exercises & Daily Tasks

- **Leadership Journal**: Write daily about your leadership experiences and lessons learned.
- **Gratitude Reflection**: Each day, note three things you are grateful for as a leader.
- **Service Challenge**: Commit to one act of service each week that uplifts others.

The Importance of Hiring a Mentor

A mentor walks with you on your leadership journey, offering wisdom, accountability, and encouragement. Their support accelerates your growth and deepens your impact.

Quote from Paolo Ben Salmi

"Your leadership power is your legacy in motion, step into it with courage and purpose." Paolo Ben Salmi

Key Takeaways

- Leadership power comes from within and grows through intentional action.
- Authenticity, resilience, and service define impactful leaders.
- Leadership is a lifelong journey of growth and contribution.
- Mentors are essential partners in your leadership development.

A big misconception of leadership that a lot of people have is that you're there to tell people what to do, leadership is simply being the conductor of an orchestra, so you're not going around picking up the violinists violin, pressing the frets showing them where they need to play. You're just letting them do their thing, but you're sort of just gently guiding… conducting them into organic flow. Because good leadership is allowing your followers to do what they do best, and conduct it. Effortless leadership is putting good people together to contribute to a bigger goal. Obviously, that's the show, but behind the scenes, you'll be there taking them through it, adjusting sounds, teaching them how to play together, first of all, and then finding the best talent that there is and cultivating that. This is what I believe is what good leadership looks like. It's just effortless leadership that really and truly is just putting good people together that you think are able to work together that can contribute to a bigger goal.

Click on this link to watch the video of the above: https://www.instagram.com/reel/C-mfIsshSWV/?igsh=MTI4b3A yaDlvdjgxbg%3D%3D

REFERENCES

References

1. Munroe, Myles. *Principles and Power of Vision*. Destiny Image Publishers, 1992.
2. Munroe, Myles. *The Spirit of Leadership*. Destiny Image Publishers, 1996.
3. Northouse, Peter G. *Leadership: Theory and Practice*. Sage Publications, 2018.
4. Kouzes, James M., and Barry Z. Posner. *The Leadership Challenge*. Jossey-Bass, 2017.
5. African Energy Week. *Youth Engagement and Leadership in Energy*. AEW Publications, 2025.
6. Additional articles, journals, and leadership case studies referenced throughout the chapters.
7. Paolo Ben Salmi, Big Question, book series, referenced throughout the chapters.

APPENDIX

Appendix

A. Kingdom Leadership Principles Summary

- Vision
- Character
- Servanthood
- Responsibility

B. Daily Leadership Planner Template

- Goal Setting
- Affirmations
- Reflection Questions

C. Recommended Reading List

- *The Power of Now* by Eckhart Tolle
- *Start with Why* by Simon Sinek
- *Mindset* by Carol Dweck
- *Developing the Leader Within You* by John Maxwell

D. Mentor Finder Resources

- Online platforms and communities for leadership mentorship
- Networking tips and events
- CFDs.

ABOUT THE
AUTHOR

Written by Paolo Ben Salmi

About the Author

Paolo Ben Salmi is a passionate mindset and leadership coach/mentor, speaker, and advocate for youth empowerment across Africa. Drawing on his extensive experience and inspired by the timeless principles of Dr. Myles Munroe, Paolo dedicates his life to helping individuals unlock their true potential through mindset transformation and character-driven leadership. He believes that every person holds the power to lead with purpose and leave a lasting legacy.

At 16, Paolo is known as the Pint Size Adventurer™. He is the founder of Adventurous Publishing House, Climate Activist who planted 10k trees in Tanzania, teen advocate, proud contributor to the Arabian Business magazine, proud contributor alongside Paolo's four siblings proud contributor alongside his four siblings at the UN SOTF Youth Consultation, ambassador for iamtheCODE, Play Seat and Water-to-Go and PlaySeat, International keynote speaker, head hunted to develop UnLtd application process, moderator, author of 15 plus books and has published over 36 books and counting under his very own publishing house called: Adventurous Publishing, he is a multiple award winner, mindset and leadership mentor, founder of the Big Question brand and book series encouraging young people to explore the world around them and embark on their own adventures: https://linktr.ee/AuthorPaolobensalmi

Below are screenshot from the Arabian Business: https://www.arabianbusiness.com/opinion/could-a-mindset-switch-be-what-the-world-needs-now

www.arabianbusiness.com

ArabianBusiness   Subscribe

Opinion

Could a 'mindset switch' be what the world needs now?

People often remember things that they need not, but forget things that are important – such as a close friend's birthday. We can change this with a four-step M.I.N.D. process that tidies up the environments within our minds

Abdul Rawuf   **Wed 20 Apr 2022**

f   in   X   ✉   ☺   G

Paolo Ben Salmi is a Publisher, Author, Public Speaker, Child Advocate, Visionary, Climate Activist, Environmental Campaigner. Founder of Adventurous Publishing & The Ben Salmis. IKAR Institute Young Leader

Written by Paolo Ben Salmi

www.arabianbusiness.com

ArabianBusiness | Subscribe | Hi Sabrina ⌄ ☰

D – Decorate

The best thing about our mind is decorations, decorate your thoughts so that whenever you think them you think positive!

Would you agree that if every movie had a positive title that we would all watch it? Well, the answer for those that have a mindset with a fertile ground is yes!

And the answer would be the opposite for those with an unfertile, negative mindset. We need a positive environment to flourish! A flower doesn't grow in a storm!

Paolo Ben Salmi is a Publisher, Author, Public Speaker, Child Advocate, Visionary, Climate Activist, Environmental Campaigner. Founder of Adventurous Publishing & The Ben Salmis. IKAR Institute Young Leader.

Written by Paolo Ben Salmi

thought is being escorted right out!

As you are reading your mind is learning and capturing information, your mind is discovering, storing, and even creating

N – Nourish

In order to sustain good thoughts you must feed them with what I would refer to as UFFT (sorry about the odd name!).

UFFT = Unconscious Foods for Thoughts. e.g., In order to sustain a negative thought, the menu it would feed on would be negative emotions such as, sadness, anger, confusion and many more! Think about what you are feeding your thoughts to sustain them?

Finally....

D – Decorate

The best thing about our mind is decorations,

Written by Paolo Ben Salmi

181

unpleasant inside you would probably say No!

Well, it's the same with your mind. Match the beautiful outside to the inside. Live in a pleasant environment. And to do that we have to look at the M.I.N.D. – a four-step process to help you create a nice interior (your mind).

M – Magnify

Would you agree that if I asked you to see words from one hundred miles away with your own eyes that it would possibly be very hard, or impossible if you will. It's the same with your mind, to see what you need and don't need, you need to magnify what's already there.

I – Identification

As an adult, when you ask for a drink that contains alcohol what question would the bartender or seller ask you? For your ID, right? We should do the same with our thoughts, actions, and even habitual actions (things that we do repetitively without realising it).

Question and interrogate that thought or that belief before you give it access to enter your mind, e.g., Shutting someone's hand in the door.

First, question whether that would be necessary. Second question how that would benefit yourself or even your friend. Finally, third give or decline

ArabianBusiness   (Subscribe)   Hi Sabrina ∨ ≡

Youth of today, leaders of tomorrow

The pandemic has kick-started the fourth industrial revolution, which means that there has been a redefining of what it means to be a leader and be the voice for those who have lost their voices

AB   Arabian Business: Latest News on the Middle East, Real Estate, Finance, and More   ⤳

But most of the time we remember the things that we shouldn't. We can start changing that by starting what I call a 'mindset switch'.

Don't worry, this mindset switch' doesn't mean you have to acquire special cables and transfer someone else's mind into yours; a 'mindset switch' means you have to take out what you don't want in your mind anymore, and exchange what you do want.

To help you better understand, think of your mind as an environment that you must live in. I bet that if I told you that you had to live in a beautiful house on the outside, but untidy and an unpleasant inside you would probably say No!

Written by Paolo Ben Salmi

183

ArabianBusiness   (Subscribe)   Hi Sabrina ⌄ ☰

We live in a world that is forever changing. As you are reading right now, it's likely that experiments are being conducted. There might even be engineers constructing new innovative inventions. But the number one thing that is drastically changing is our minds.

As you are reading, your mind is learning and capturing information, your mind is discovering, storing, and even creating.

We might not be able to change the world, but the one thing we can change and evolve are our minds. We continuously capture information, but just because we capture information, does not mean that we will remember it.

It's the same way you remember a news title (because of letters in bold and captivating words) and forget your friend's birthday.

You don't forget your friend's birthday because you don't care, you forget your friend's birthday because the world has conditioned us to believe that other things are more important.

The media has a way of capturing your attention through words such as attention, warning, breaking news, and caution!

Written by Paolo Ben Salmi

KEEP IN TOUCH

Written by Paolo Ben Salmi

Mentoring, Mastermind & Workshop Opportunities etc

Ready to elevate your leadership skills and mindset?

Join Paolo's exclusive mentorship programs, masterminds, and workshops designed to accelerate your learning curve and connect you with a community of successful traders. These programs offer personalised mentoring/coaching, advanced strategies, and accountability to help you reach your financial goals faster.

Contact:
Email: info@dreamingbigtogether.com
LinkedIn: Paolo Ben Salmi
Linktree: https://linktr.ee/authorpaolobensalmi
Instagram: @AuthorPaoloBenSalmi

Take the next step and work directly with me to unlock your full trading potential.

www.ingramcontent.com/pod-product-compliance
Lightning Source LLC
Chambersburg PA
CBHW060556200326
41521CB00007B/591